Animals That Live in the Forest/
Animales del bosque

Opossums/Zarigüeyas

By JoAnn Early Macken

Reading Consultant: Jeanne Clidas, Ph.D.
Director, Roberts Wesleyan College Literacy Clinic

WEEKLY READER®
PUBLISHING

Please visit our web site at **www.garethstevens.com**.
For a free catalog describing our list of high-quality books,
call 1-877-542-2595 (USA) or 1-800-387-3178 (Canada).
Our fax: 1-877-542-2596

Library of Congress Cataloging-in-Publication Data

Macken, JoAnn Early, 1953–
    [Opossums. Spanish & English]
    Opossums = Zarigüeyas / by JoAnn Early Macken; reading consultant, Jeanne Clidas.
       p. cm. — (Animals that live in the forest = Animales del bosque)
    Includes bibliographical references and index.
    English and Spanish; translated from the English.
    ISBN-10: 1-4339-2437-4   ISBN-13: 978-1-4339-2437-8 (lib. bdg.)
    ISBN-10: 1-4339-2488-9   ISBN-13: 978-1-4339-2488-0 (soft cover)
    1. Opossums–Juvenile literature. I. Title. II. Title: Zarigüeya.
QL737.M34M3418   2009
599.2'76–dc22
                                                                                                      2009008342

This edition first published in 2010 by
Weekly Reader® Books
An Imprint of Gareth Stevens Publishing
1 Reader's Digest Road
Pleasantville, NY 10570-7000 USA

Copyright © 2010 by Gareth Stevens, Inc.

Executive Managing Editor: Lisa M. Herrington
Senior Editor: Barbara Bakowski
Cover Designers: Jennifer Ryder-Talbot and Studio Montage
Production: Studio Montage
Translators: Tatiana Acosta and Guillermo Gutiérrez
Library Consultant: Carl Harvey, Library Media Specialist, Noblesville, Indiana

Photo credits: Cover, p. 19 Shutterstock; pp. 1, 9, 13, 15 © Steve Maslowski/Visuals Unlimited;
p. 5 © Gary Meszaros/Visuals Unlimited; pp. 7, 11 © Alan and Sandy Carey; p. 17 © Michael H. Francis;
p. 21 © William Grenfell/Visuals Unlimited

All rights reserved. No part of this book may be reproduced, stored in a retrieval system,
or transmitted in any form or by any means, electronic, mechanical, photocopying, recording,
or otherwise, without the prior written permission of the copyright holder. For permission, contact
permissions@gspub.com.

Printed in the United States of America

1 2 3 4 5 6 7 8 9 14 13 12 11 10 09

Table of Contents

Baby Opossums................4
Tiny Climbers................10
Nighttime Hunters................14
Glossary................22
For More Information................23
Index................24

- - - - - - - - - - - - - -

Contenido

Crías de zarigüeya................4
Pequeñas trepadoras................10
Cazadoras nocturnas................14
Glosario................22
Más información................23
Índice................24

Boldface words appear in the glossary./
Las palabras en **negrita** aparecen en el glosario.

Baby Opossums

A mother opossum carries her babies in her **pouch**. The pouch is like a pocket. It may hold twelve tiny babies. They have no hair. They cannot see or hear.

- - - - - - - - - - - - - - - -

Crías de zarigüeya

Una madre zarigüeya lleva a sus crías en el **marsupio**. El marsupio es como un bolsillo. En él caben hasta doce diminutas crías. Las crías no tienen pelo. No pueden ver ni oír.

The babies drink milk from their mother. After about two months, they open their eyes. They look out at the world. They crawl out of the pouch.

Las crías beben la leche de la madre. Después de unos dos meses, abren los ojos. Echan un vistazo al mundo y salen del marsupio.

Baby opossums stay near their mother. She shows them how to find food and climb trees. She carries them on her back.

- - - - - - - - - - - - - - -

Las crías de zarigüeya se quedan cerca de su madre. Ésta les enseña cómo buscar comida y trepar a los árboles. La madre lleva a las crías sobre el lomo.

Tiny Climbers

Opossums have long noses with whiskers. Their fur is gray and white.

- - - - - - - - - - - - - - -

Pequeñas trepadoras

Las zarigüeyas tienen una nariz larga con vibrisas. Su pelaje es gris y blanco.

Opossums are good climbers. They hold on to branches with their sharp **claws** and long tails. Babies can even hang by their tails!

- - - - - - - - - - - - - - -

Las zarigüeyas son buenas trepadoras. Se sujetan a las ramas con sus afiladas **garras** y su larga cola. ¡Las crías pueden incluso colgarse de la cola!

claws/
garras

Nighttime Hunters

Opossums are **nocturnal** (NAHK-ter-nahl). They are active at night. They hunt for food. They climb trees to escape from danger.

- - - - - - - - - - - - - - -

Cazadoras nocturnas

Las zarigüeyas son **nocturnas**. Están activas durante la noche. Salen de caza en busca de comida. En caso de peligro, trepan a los árboles.

Opossums sniff to find their food. They eat grass and fruit. They also eat eggs, insects, and small animals.

- - - - - - - - - - - - - - -

Para encontrar comida, las zarigüeyas usan el olfato. Se alimentan de hierba y frutas. También comen huevos, insectos y otros animales pequeños.

egg/huevo

During the day, opossums sleep in **dens**. A den may be in a log or a tree stump. It may be an old den from another animal.

Durante el día, las zarigüeyas duermen en su **madriguera**. La madriguera puede estar en un tronco hueco. También puede ser la antigua madriguera de otro animal.

den/
madriguera

An opossum in danger may stay very still. Other animals think it is dead. They leave it alone.

- - - - - - - - - - - - - - - -

A veces, una zarigüeya en peligro se queda muy quieta. Otros animales piensan que está muerta y la dejan en paz.

Fast Facts/Datos básicos

Length/ Longitud	about 3 feet (1 meter) nose to tail/ unos 3 pies (1 metro) de nariz a cola
Weight/ Peso	about 14 pounds (6 kilograms)/ unas 14 libras (6 kilogramos)
Diet/ Dieta	insects, birds, small animals, grass, eggs, and fruit/insectos, pájaros, animales pequeños, hierba, huevos y frutas
Average life span/ Promedio de vida	up to 4 years/ hasta 4 años

Glossary/Glosario

claws: sharp, curved nails on an animal's foot

dens: places where wild animals rest or live

nocturnal: active mostly at night

pouch: a body part that is like a pocket

- - - - - - - - - - - - - - - - - - -

garras: uñas afiladas

madrigueras: lugares donde descansan o viven algunos animales salvajes

marsupio: parte del cuerpo similar a un bolsillo

nocturno: que está activo sobre todo de noche

For More Information/Más información

Books/Libros

Opossums. Backyard Animals (series). Christine Webster (Weigl Publishers, 2007)

What Forest Animals Eat/¿Qué comen los animales del bosque? Nature's Food Chains (series). Joanne Mattern (Gareth Stevens, 2007)

Web Sites/Páginas web

The National Opossum Society/La Sociedad Nacional de la Zarigüeya
www.opossum.org
Visit this site for lots of interesting facts and fun photos./ Visiten esta página web para conocer muchos datos interesantes y ver divertidas fotografías.

Virginia Opossum/Zarigüeya de Virginia
www.enchantedlearning.com/subjects/mammals/marsupial/ vaopossumprintout.shtml
Find a diagram you can print out and color./Busquen un diagrama que pueden imprimir y colorear.

Publisher's note to educators and parents: Our editors have carefully reviewed these web sites to ensure that they are suitable for children. Many web sites change frequently, however, and we cannot guarantee that a site's future contents will continue to meet our high standards of quality and educational value. Be advised that children should be closely supervised whenever they access the Internet.

Nota de la editorial a los padres y educadores: Nuestros editores han revisado con cuidado las páginas web para asegurarse de que son apropiadas para niños. Sin embargo, muchas páginas web cambian con frecuencia, y no podemos garantizar que sus contenidos futuros sigan conservando nuestros elevados estándares de calidad y de interés educativo. Tengan en cuenta que los niños deben ser supervisados atentamente siempre que accedan a Internet.

Index/Índice

babies 4, 6, 8, 12	dens 18	pouches 4, 6
claws 12	food 6, 8, 14, 16	sleeping 18
climbing 8, 12, 14	fur 10	tails 12
danger 14, 20	noses 10	whiskers 10

---

colas 12	garras 12	pelaje 10
comida 6, 8, 14, 16	madrigueras 18	peligro 14, 20
crías 4, 6, 8, 12	marsupios 4, 6	trepar 8, 12, 14
dormir 18	narices 10	vibrisas 10

About the Author
JoAnn Early Macken is the author of two rhyming picture books, *Sing-Along Song* and *Cats on Judy*, and more than 80 nonfiction books for children. Her poems have appeared in several children's magazines. She lives in Wisconsin with her husband and their two sons.

Información sobre la autora
JoAnn Early Macken ha escrito dos libros de rimas con ilustraciones, *Sing-Along Song* y *Cats on Judy*, y más de ochenta libros de no ficción para niños. Sus poemas han sido publicados en varias revistas infantiles. Vive en Wisconsin con su esposo y sus dos hijos.

```
HKENX  + SP
       599
       .276
       M
```

MACKEN, JOANN EARLY
    OPOSSUMS

KENDALL
01/10